Kids' Bathroom Book
WHODUNITS

By
JIM SUKACH

Illustrated by
LUCY CORVINO

Sterling Publishing Co., Inc.
New York

Library of Congress
Cataloging-in-Publication Data available
2   4   6   8   10   9   7   5   3

Published by Sterling Publishing Co., Inc.
387 Park Avenue South, New York, NY 10016
© 2003 by James Sukach
Excerpted from *Baffling Whodunit Puzzles* © 1996
by James Richard Sukach; *Clever Quicksolve*
Whodunit Puzzles © 1999 by James Richard Sukach;
Great Quicksolve Whodunit Puzzles © 1998 by James Richard Sukach;
Challenging Whodunit Puzzles © 1997 by James Richard Sukach.
Distributed in Canada by Sterling Publishing
c/o Canadian Manda Group, One Atlantic Avenue, Suite 105
Toronto, Ontario, Canada M6K 3E7
Distributed in Great Britain and Europe by Chris Lloyd at Orca Book
Services, Stanley House, Fleets Lane, Poole BH15 3AJ, England

Manufactured in China

Sterling ISBN 1-4027-0719-3

Contents

1. Small Change

Dr. J.L. Quicksolve and his son Junior were out for a motorcycle ride when they decided to stop by the police station to see their friend Sergeant Rebekah Shurshot.

When they walked into her office, she was talking to a short, bald-headed man who seemed to be very upset. A young man Dr. Quicksolve did not recognize was putting money into the pay phone in the corner. He wore handcuffs.

"Are you busy?" Dr. Quicksolve asked Sergeant Shurshot.

"Yes," she answered, "but maybe you and Junior can help. She introduced them to Mr. Moneysave, the bald man. Then

she explained that Mr. Moneysave's house had been burglarized and the man on the phone was caught in his yard. She said he had been talking to his lawyer for 20 minutes. She also explained that jewelry and a valuable coin collection had been stolen. The jewelry had been found in the yard, but not the coin collection.

"The coins were actually more valuable than the jewelry," Mr. Moneysave explained. "I specialize in Barber dimes. I had some from 1892 to 1916. They are worth thousands of dollars!"

Finally, the man in handcuffs came over to where they were talking. "My lawyer's gonna get me out of here in a few minutes," he said.

"Is your lawyer here in town?" Dr. Quicksolve asked.

"Yes, Cheater and Sewer. Their office is just two blocks away."

"Book him, call the phone company and let's go to lunch," Dr. Quicksolve said.

"What evidence do you have?" the young man protested.

"I can answer that one," Junior said.

What had Dr. Quicksolve and Junior figured out?

Answer on page 85.

8

2. High Voltage

Dan Voltage's name was all over the newspapers. This local eighth-grade science teacher had just discovered an inexpensive way to turn water into gasoline. His spirits were high, and he was certain to make millions of dollars with his new process. Now his name would be in the paper for another reason. He had been kidnapped.

Dr. J.L. Quicksolve, his son Junior, and Lieutenant Rootumout were at Voltage's house talking with Mrs. Voltage. Dr. Quicksolve and Junior had been watching a soccer game in a drizzling rain when Lieutenant Rootumout paged the detective. They had come straight from the soccer game. "When I got home I found this note," Mrs. Voltage explained.

Lieutenant Rootumout read the note: "If he gives us the formula, we will let him go. Do not try to find us."

"He was here a few hours ago when I left to go shopping," Mrs. Voltage said. "As I drove away I saw our neighbor, Brace Yaseph, and another man pull into our driveway in a van."

11

Dr. Quicksolve walked from room to room, looking for clues. On the kitchen table was a bottle of lemon juice and a glass filled with what looked like lemonade. If there had been ice, it had melted. There was a basket containing grapes, bananas, and apples. Next to that lay a sheet of paper and a toothpick. In the living room he noticed an ashtray filled with cigarette stubs. "Does your husband smoke?" he asked.

"No, he never smokes," Mrs. Voltage answered.

"If someone has a match, we might find Mr. Voltage," Junior said from behind them. Lieutenant Rootumout looked puzzled. Dr. Quicksolve smiled.

12 ◯ **What did Junior have in mind?**

Answer on pages 85–86.

3. Early Morning Crime

"Look at this!" Shortstop, Quicksolve Junior's best friend, was upset. He was pointing to his locker, which had been so badly damaged it could not be closed. "Someone broke into my locker and stole my jacket!"

Junior surveyed the scene. The locker had been forced open with some kind of a prybar. It must have taken a while. About a dozen or more red pistachio shells lay in front of the locker. One or two shells were inside it. An empty cola bottle was on the floor.

"It looks like the culprit had a snack while he pried it open," Junior said. "Yeah. That stuff wasn't there when I went to class," Shortstop said.

"Second hour hasn't started yet, so it obviously happened during first hour," Junior thought out loud.

They went to the principal and reported what had happened. He said several lockers had been broken into in the past week. Junior suggested he question everyone who was out of class during first hour. The principal called the teachers over the public address system, and four kids were sent to the office.

14

Junior peeked at the four suspects from the principal's office. He knew all four. Prissy Powers was the cutest girl on the cheerleading squad. She had to brush her hair and check her makeup at

least once an hour. Dennie Dos, the computer expert in the school, sat twiddling his thumbs. John Bigdood had a reputation as a bully, but he had never been caught stealing. He sat there with his band gloves on, drumsticks in hand, playing an imaginary drum. Art Full was doodling on a notepad. No one looked happy about being sent to the office.

16

Junior turned to the principal. "I think I know who did it, and I can prove it," he said.

Who? How?

Answer on page 86.

4. Hopalong

Junior looked around at the small Texas town in amazement as he rode slowly down the main street on the back of his father's motorcycle. A large banner stretched across the street said, "Hopalong Cassidy Days."

"This looks like a town straight out of the Old West!" he said to his dad.

Dr. J.L. Quicksolve turned his head and said, "It sure does, except for the cars and the neon lights."

Junior noticed there were even horses tied up in front of several places, including a saloon, where a crowd had gathered. The Old

West picture was spoiled, though, by the flashing lights of a yellow ambulance and a police car with a large gold star on the door. Dr. Quicksolve pulled up, parked his motorcycle, and went to see what happened. He expected that the man he was here to see, his old friend, Sheriff Sam Sixshot, would be on the scene.

18

He was right. A man named Slim had been shot in the back in front of the saloon. Dusty Throte was the only one who saw anything.

"I was walking toward the saloon, about half a block away. I saw a guy in a black outfit come out of the saloon, turn right, draw a gun, and shoot Slim down just as he lifted his foot into the stirrup to get on his horse," Dusty explained, pointing to a white horse tied to a hitching post about 20 feet from the saloon.

"That's not much of a description," Sheriff Sixshot said, "considering half the men in town are wearing black outfits today to celebrate Hopalong Cassidy Days."

Junior looked around, a little dis- appointed in himself for not noticing all the men in black cowboy outfits and white hats. Then he perked up and said, matter-of-factly, "But we don't really need to know anything else, do we Dad?"

What had Junior figured out?

20

Answer on page 86.

5. Five-Finger Discount

Junior, Shortstop, and Prissy Powers were sitting in a restaurant at the mall, sipping colas. John Bigdood and Bobby Socks had been sitting in the next booth. Suddenly John got up and said, "Let's go." As Bobby stood up, John twiddled his fingers and said, "Time for a little five-finger discount."

Junior, Shortstop, and Prissy pretended not to hear. "Let's follow them," Junior said.

They followed the two suspects from a distance, stopping to look at things, but not going into any stores. When John and Bobby entered the Metal Bop Music Shop, they followed.

The threesome pretended to browse, pulling out disks or cassettes and looking at the songs. John Bigdood went up to the clerk at the cash register. Bobby stayed at the opposite side of the store. John held a CD by the Metal Road Frogs. "Do you have 'Carrion Cousins' by the Metal Road Frogs?" he asked loudly. The clerk said no, and John said, "Oh, okay," and quickly turned and walked out of the store. The alarm screamed! John walked back in. "Sorry," he said, and laid the CD on the counter. He walked out again, and he and Bobby walked away.

Junior went up to the clerk and said, "Call security."

What did Junior suspect?

Answer on pages 86–87.

23

6. I'd Rather Owe You

Junior and Shortstop were playing soccer in the small neighborhood park. They had brought Copper, Junior's retriever, to the park for a little exercise. Junior had let Copper off his leash so he could run a little.

24

Looking up the street, the boys saw a couple of people walking toward them, obviously arguing. It was Prissy Powers and Lyle Loppitt, a new boy in the neighborhood. They could see Lyle was sipping a frozen soft drink through a straw from a Super Slop Icy cup, the kind sold at the Stop-n-Hop convenience store three blocks down on the corner. Lyle walked away, apparently in a huff, crossed the street, and disappeared down an alley.

When Prissy walked up to Junior and Shortstop, she was obviously upset. "Don't ever lend money to that guy," she said.

"What happened?" Junior asked.

"Lyle asked me to lend him a dollar for a Super Slop Icy cup a few minutes ago. I only had a five-dollar bill, so I gave him that. I told him I would meet him here to get the change."

"Did he give you your change back?" Shortstop asked.

"No. He said Copper attacked him and knocked him down, and he lost the money," she said.

"Copper attacked him?" Junior asked.

26

"I told him Copper doesn't attack people. He said they wrestled on the ground a few minutes before he realized Copper was just playing, but the money was lost. He said it blew away and he couldn't find it. I said I needed the money. He said, 'I'd rather owe it to you than cheat you out of it.' I don't believe his story," Prissy said.

"No. It can't be true," Junior said.

27

Apart from the fact that Junior knew his dog would not jump on anyone, how did he know Lyle's story was not true?

Answer on page 87.

7. Frontiersman

Sergeant Shurshot had talked Dr. J. L. Quicksolve and Junior into hiking with her and the talkative Benjamin Clayborn Blowhard. Junior led them along the narrow path of the nature trail. Blowhard, in his Rough Riders-style cowboy hat with one side pinned up, talked continuously. "The way you are leading us along, Junior, reminds me of an ancestor of mine. He was a famous frontiersman and scout. His name was Kit Carson. A lot of people don't know about a lot of the heroes of American history," Blowhard said.

"I know about Kit Carson," Junior said.

"He was quite a man," Blowhard continued. "He was a pony express rider, racing across the countryside, hopping from one horse to another. Then he became a scout for the army. He won the Congressional Medal of Honor for bravery."

"Congressional Medal of Honor?" said Dr. Quicksolve.

"Then he toured with Buffalo Bill's Wild West Show and was a scout for Lieutenant Custer. In fact, he died at Custer's Last Stand," Blowhard said.

"Your story sounds confused," Junior said.

"You mean confusing," Sergeant Shurshot said.

"That too," Junior replied.

30 **What did Junior mean?**

Answer on pages 87–88.

8. Egyptian Mystery

Aunt Toni met Junior and his twin cousins, Flora and Fauna, at the airport. The girls were very excited about their first trip to New York City, and Junior loved to visit his Aunt Toni. The three kids, with their big smiles, were easy to spot as they came off the plane. Aunt Toni, wearing a long dress and standing next to her uniformed chauffeur, Pete, was even easier to spot.

Junior helped Pete load the bags into the limo, and they headed straight to the Metropolitan Museum of Art, where a King Tut exhibition was on display. The kids loved seeing the mummies and all the gold. The girls were amazed at the size of Tut's gold earrings, which required holes in his ears big enough to stick a finger through. Junior, who'd been studying Egypt in preparation for the trip, was amazed by everything.

When they stopped to eat lunch at the museum restaurant, Flora commented about all the armed guards they had seen. "Well, the treasure is very important to Egypt," Aunt Toni explained. Then she pulled out her lighter, flicked it on, and paused. She clicked the lighter closed suddenly and said, "And the murder, of course." That got everyone's attention.

32

Aunt Toni said that a curator at the museum had taken a few pieces of gold jewelry home to study. "He was found dead in his apartment right in my building, apartment 202. He was slumped over a plate of spaghetti. The jewelry was gone. There were three small strands of spaghetti on the table by his hand that looked as if they had been purposely arranged to look like two nines. The police thought it might be a message from the killer or a clue from the victim—a telephone number or something."

"A room number?" Flora suggested.

"A special code?" Fauna asked.

"They have not found the jewels. The police are still searching everyone who leaves the building," Aunt Toni said. "People are getting angry. The police will have to stop that pretty soon."

34

"The jewels are probably in the next apartment," Junior said.

If you know what Junior was talking about, you've been studying Egypt too!

Answer on pages 88–89.

9. Junior's Mystery Puzzle

As they drove away from the Guggenheim Museum in Aunt Toni's limousine, Junior opened his notebook. He said, "I've written a mystery puzzle. See if you can figure it out. It's a murder confession."

"Who is confessing?" Flora asked.

"I didn't give him a name," Junior said.

"Let's call him Lenny," Fauna said.

"The only Lenny I know," Flora said, "never confessed to anything."

Junior held the letter so his cousins could see it as he read it to them:

June 31

I have been sitting here for hours in this nowhere café. I watch the rain pattering against the window. It has rained for days. It is ceaseless, like the pain I feel for what I've done. My glasses fog, and my eyes tear. I sip my coffee, and I write this confession. I killed her out of jealousy. It was not my brother. He was out of town yesterday.

I went to her house in my brother's convertible so no one would suspect me. I put the top up as I pulled out of the driveway so no one would see me. I knocked on her door, and she let me in. Though I was angry, I smiled. Then I shot her. She fell to the floor. I kept shooting. I loaded a second clip into my revolver and continued shooting. I just went crazy. I don't know why.

I went straight to my brother's apartment and told him what I did. He said he would protect me. He would take the blame. I cannot let him do that.

"I know one mistake," Flora said.

"I know two," Fauna said.

"I know three," said Flora.

"That's five!" they said together.

38 Junior was a little confused by his cousins' responses, but he had to confess they were right.

Did you find five problems with the confession?

Answer on page 89.

10. A Young Hero

Junior Quicksolve walked into the general store, took two licorice sticks from the jar on the counter, and left the money so Uncle Anvil would not have to get up from his game of checkers.

Uncle Anvil wasn't in a very good mood because it was one of those rare moments when he was losing a checker game to Slim Harmony.

39

Then Uncle Anvil's bad mood suddenly slipped away like a Midwestern thunderstorm on a windy day. He was all smiles and sunshine as he reached the board and jumped four of Slim's checkers.

"I wish you wouldn't do that." Slim snorted.

Junior sat down to watch the game. It didn't take long for Anvil to begin telling another story about Junior's dad, Dr. J.L. Quicksolve, when he was a young boy.

"Your dad was a hero in town when he was about eight years old," Uncle Anvil began. "He was on the porch sipping lemonade one hot summer day. Two kids were jumping rope and playing with a hula hoop, and some men were digging a ditch along the road in front of the house. Your dad went inside to get some cookies for the younger kids. He heard the boy scream, and ran out to find that the four-year-old girl had fallen into the ditch. The men apparently had gone to lunch."

"Was she hurt?" Junior asked.

"She'd sprained her wrist from the fall, but she was okay—just scared. Your dad lay on his stomach and tried to reach down to her. Their fingers just barely touched. The biggest problem was that the sides of the deep hole were loose and could cave in on her at any minute. The boy ran for help, and the little girl was screaming down in that hole. Your dad kept his cool, though. He couldn't wait for help, but he knew what to do."

"The jump rope," Slim suggested, as he moved a checker.

42 Uncle Anvil, who had not taken his mind off the game, jumped Slim's checker and said, "She couldn't hold her weight with the sprained wrist. She was too scared to do anything too complicated."

"I know!" Junior said.

What had Junior figured out?

Answer on pages 89–90.

11. Australian Adventure

Dr. J.L. Quicksolve, Sergeant Rebekah Shurshot, Junior Quicksolve, and Benjamin Clayborn Blowhard sat in a restaurant for afternoon tea. Dr. Quicksolve drank coffee, and Junior took the opportunity to have a banana split. Benjamin Clayborn Blowhard was telling stories of his adventures, danger, and daring.

Junior enjoyed Blowhard's stories. To him they were verbal cartoons. Dr. Quicksolve was trying to be pleasant, relax, and avoid a headache. Sergeant Rebekah Shurshot was fascinated. "I was deep in the Australian Outback, alone and making camp along a rushing river, when something frightened my horse and caused him to run, abandoning me in the middle of wild and dangerous country," Blowhard said. "It didn't take long to figure out what had scared the horse. A huge bear came storming out of the brush, bent on having me for dinner and not as a guest. I dove into the river thinking the bear would not follow me into the strong current of white water. Clinging to a rock, I watched the bear pace back and forth, deciding what to do.

"Suddenly something grabbed my boot and pulled me under the foaming water. Below the surface, desperate for air, I realized a five-foot alligator was also inviting me for dinner. I pulled out my knife and struggled with the beast as the current bounced us along the rocks, pulling us downstream.

"Finally, the alligator had enough, released my boot, and was swept away. I struggled to the shore. Fortunately, the bear gave up, too, and was gone when I dragged myself back to camp,

where I fell face down into my tent and slept for three hours."

"Wow!" Sergeant Shurshot said.

Junior laughed and dug into his ice cream.

Dr. Quicksolve just shook his head.

What was wrong with Blowhard's story?

Answer on page 90.

12. Shortstop's Business

Junior Quicksolve parked his bike by the sign that said "Shortstop's Grass Cutting Service." He walked up to the front porch of his friend's house, and the door opened even before he could ring the doorbell. "You said on the phone that you had a problem," Junior said, noticing Shortstop's neighbor, Stephen Spekoldot.

"Yes," Stephen answered before Shortstop could get a word out. "I think it was John Bigdood!"

"What was John Bigdood?" Junior asked, turning to Shortstop for the answer.

Shortstop led Junior into his room and pointed to a small safe standing wide open on the floor. "That," Shortstop said. "Somebody apparently came into the house while I was at my computer. He opened my safe and took 130-some dollars."

"Thirty-five," Stephen corrected.

"That's right," Shortstop said. "I counted $135. I was at the computer adding up my earnings and figuring how much I owed the guys who help me. I always do that when I bring money home."

"Why do you think it was John Bigdood?" Junior asked Stephen.

"I saw somebody. It looked like him, but I only saw his back."

"You saw him leave the house?" Junior asked.

"No, I saw him at the safe. I was up there, looking around with my telescope." Stephen pointed out the window and up to the window in the next house where a long telescope on a tripod stuck outside. "I could see Shortstop at his computer, too. It looked suspicious, so I came down and ran in the front door to warn Shortstop.

John must have heard me and run out the back door."

"Has John been here lately?" Junior asked.

"Yes, he was here yesterday. He said his dad and mom wanted me to cut their grass while they were on vacation. But how could he know my combination?" Shortstop said.

"I think that's one of the questions we just have to look up the answers to," Junior said.

What did Junior mean by that?

Answer on page 90.

13. Classroom Crime

Junior sat in Principal Paddlebottom's office. Junior's friend, Shortstop, sat next to him. Bobby Socks sat across the room from them. Mrs. Spellbinder, Junior's teacher, stood talking to Mr. Paddlebottom. She told the principal that she came into school this morning, unlocked her room, put her purse in her classroom closet, and went to the teachers' workroom. She noticed Bobby Socks was painting the wall in the hall outside her room, but she did not think she needed to lock the door. When she got back, her closet door was open, and money was gone from her purse.

"Bobby was painting over some things that should not have been written on the wall in the first place," Mr. Paddlebottom said. Then he turned to Junior and Shortstop. "You two came in early today?"

"Yes," Junior said. "We saw Mrs. Spellbinder walking toward the teachers' workroom."

"And what else?" Mr. Paddlebottom asked.

Shortstop gulped nervously and said, "We saw Bobby Socks go into Mrs. Spellbinder's classroom. He came out a minute later and started painting again."

"Did you go into Mrs. Spellbinder's room, Bobby?" Mr. Paddlebottom asked, turning to look at him.

53

"I was in there just a minute, like Shortstop said," Bobby replied. "I washed a little paint off my hands. I wasn't in there long enough to do

anything else. Why don't you search Shortstop? He might have gone into the room when my back was turned," Bobby said.

"No one else has been in your room yet?" Mr. Paddlebottom asked Mrs. Spellbinder.

"I locked it after I saw the money was missing just a few minutes ago. I don't think anyone else has come into the building yet," Mrs. Spellbinder said.

Junior spoke up. "I think we can tell easily if Bobby is telling the truth."

What did Junior mean?

Answer on pages 90–91

55

14. Strikeout

Dr. J.L. Quicksolve and Junior were meeting Fred Fraudstop for lunch. Fred said he had to stop and question a man about a burglary at the Strikeout Sportscard Shop. Dr. Quicksolve decided to go with him because Junior was a baseball card collector and would be interested in the shop, not to mention Quicksolve's curiosity about the burglary.

"We were broken into overnight," Homer Hitter, the shop owner, told them. "They took a bunch of cards, but mostly money," he said, showing them the back door, which had been jimmied open, and the empty moneybox. "We close late, so I usually take the money to the bank in the morning."

"Did you lock up last night?" Dr. Quicksolve asked him. Junior was looking at

a display of Mickey Mantle cards.
He showed his dad the 1953 rookie card that
had a price of $300 on it. "Save your money," Dr.
Quicksolve said.

"No, my clerk, Art Dunn, closed up last night. He always closes up.
He bolts the back door and goes out the front. I let him have
his own key. I don't think he would do anything like this."

Then he noticed Junior looking at the cards. "You like
Mickey Mantle?" he asked Junior. He reached below the
counter and brought out a card that showed Mantle standing at
the left side of the plate as if he were waiting for a pitch. Without all
those injuries he would have been the Home Run King."

"What do you think of the Strikeout Sportscard
Shop?" Fred asked Junior as they walked out
onto the sidewalk.

58

"I don't think I'd buy anything from that guy," Junior said, "and you probably should doubt what he tells you about the robbery."

Why does Junior mistrust Homer?

Answer on page 91.

15. Socks

Bobby Socks looked menacing sitting in Mr. Paddlebottom's office when Junior and Kimberly Kay walked into the principal's office. Bobby wore his jeans tucked into baseball socks just below his knees. Most kids thought it looked funny. That suited Bobby fine because he used every excuse he could think of to start a fight. He had beaten up almost every boy in school at one time or another over some imagined insult. Junior was one of the few boys Bobby would not mess with, though Junior figured Bobby was afraid to pick on the son of the famous Dr. J.L. Quicksolve. It was as if he had something to hide and was afraid Junior would figure it out. He was right.

Kimberly's new bicycle had been stolen from her garage yesterday afternoon. She was sure she had seen Bobby in his baseball

60

uniform pushing her bike away. Mr. Paddlebottom wanted to talk to Kimberly and Bobby before he called Bobby's parents or the police. Kimberly had asked Junior to go with her to the office for moral support.

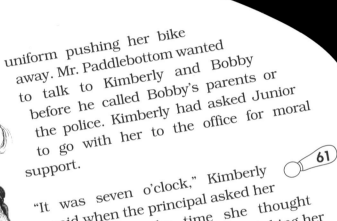

"It was seven o'clock," Kimberly said when the principal asked her the time she thought she saw Bobby taking her bike. "I was looking out the front door for my girlfriend. Her dad was going to take us shopping."

"I was playing baseball in the park at seven," Bobby said. "We were playing those bums from Jackson. We were just getting our last bats. We were ahead five to nothing when I hit my second home run of the game. Then I walked home with Michael Thomas. You can ask him."

62 "You can't believe Bobby's story, Mr. Paddlebottom," Junior said to the principal.

Why doesn't Junior believe Bobby is telling the truth?

Answer on page 91.

16. Buz

"I like doing puzzles, solving mysteries, and stuff like that," Junior explained to his grandfather Phineas Quicksolve, as they sat at the breakfast table. Junior spoke between bites, methodically shoveling away at the stack of pancakes Grandma Quicksolve made for him.

"We've got a mystery," Grandpa said, "the mystery of the missing tea." He went on to explain that Grandma made sun tea that she left on an upside down crate in the backyard each morning. About twice a week it disappeared. Grandpa suspected Buz Stinger, the boy next door, because he had seen him out in the field behind their house two or three times on days when the tea was missing.

After breakfast they went out back to check on the jar of tea Grandma had put out that morning. It was gone.

"There's Buz," Grandpa said, pointing to a boy out in the field walking away from them.

64 Junior walked fast to catch up to the boy. He avoided running so Buz would not think he was being chased and run away. As Junior got closer, he could see Buz had a jar in his hand. It was empty.

"What are you doing?" Junior asked, trying to sound friendly.

"I'm catching bees for my collection," Buz said, looking around as if searching for a little victim. "I almost got that yellow jacket," he

said, indicating a large black-and-yellow-striped bee several yards out of reach.

"Do you know a lot about bees?" Junior asked.

"Oh, yes. I study them. I just need that yellow jacket and I'll have an example of all the kinds you see around here. By the way, I'm Buz Stinger. Who are you?"

"I'm Junior Quicksolve, the guy who caught you stealing my grandma's tea," Junior replied.

Why is Junior so sure Buz stole the tea?

Answer on pages 91–92.

17. Shadow Heart Trail

"We'll go in small groups, leaving every 20 minutes. If you keep quiet as you hike, you'll see more wildlife," Junior's science teacher, Mr. Crucible, explained to the class as they prepared to begin their nature hike. "Remember," he said, "this is called Shadow Heart Trail because it goes north for two miles through a thick forest of pine trees and then forks left and right into the tough, rocky terrain. You can go either way, because each trail circles back and straightens out at an angle to bring you right back here. The trails make a heart shape. You can't get lost either way. Each group will have a walkie-talkie to call me if you have any problems."

Junior and his friends Shortstop, Danny Dos, and Prissy Powers were in the second group. They waited in the warmth of the early morning sun, checking their backpacks, lunches, and canteens. The first group disappeared into the woods. When about 20 minutes had passed, Junior's group headed into the woods with Mr. Crucible.

Their eyes adjusted to the shadowy darkness of the woods. They stopped to pull jackets and sweaters out of their backpacks because of the cool temperatures under the tall pines.

Suddenly, a voice cracked weakly over the small device. "Help," it said. "We're about two and a half miles out. We climbed a hill, and the sun was bright in our eyes. Kimberly stepped off the trail and fell into a ravine. She hurt her leg badly. Please..."

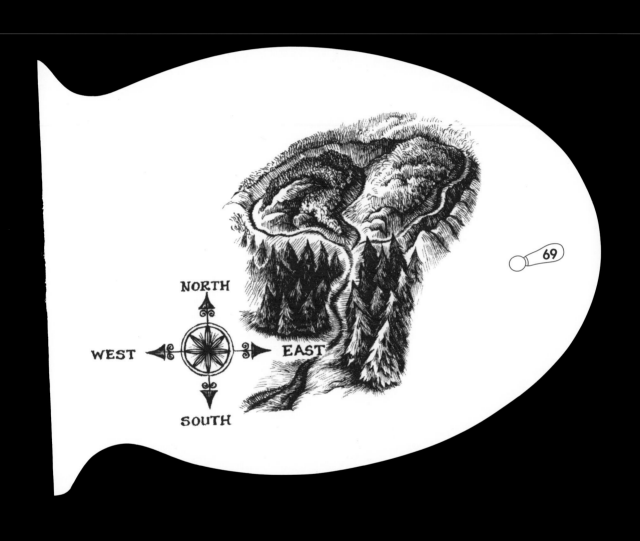

WEST • EAST • NORTH • SOUTH

69

The voice faded away.

Mr. Crucible tried to get more information, but the walkie-talkie was not working. "Let's hurry," he said. The group began to jog through the woods.

Finally they came out into the bright sunlight to a fork in the road.

"Now which way?" Mr. Crucible asked, as he looked left and right down the two trails.

"This way," Junior replied, heading to the right without hesitation.

How did Junior know which way to go?

Answer on page 92.

18. The Real McCoy

The men were in the den sipping coffee and root beer. Dr. J.L. Quicksolve had invited several friends for dinner. Since Benjamin Clayborn Blowhard was making his nest on Sergeant Rebekah Shurshot's couch for the week, he was also invited. As usual, Blowhard was doing the talking—this time about his ancestors.

71

"The men on my father's side were adventurers like I am," he said. He had spoken of that side of his family before. According to him, his family spread across the globe, meeting and aiding, instructing, or encouraging famous people.

"My mother's side was a little more stable," he went on, "living and prospering in the beautiful state of Virginia. Their name was McCoy. In fact, the expression 'the real McCoy' came from the honesty and integrity of my great-grandfather McCoy who was once nominated for governor."

Dr. Quicksolve almost choked on his coffee. Captain Reelumin, Lieutenant Rootumout, and Fred Fraudstop listened attentively. Fred was hoping for the chance to talk about his ancestors. His chances were slim. Blowhard seemed to have an endless supply of air and continued talking without the usual necessity of taking a breath.

"Why don't you tell him, Dad?" Junior whispered.

What does Junior think Dr. Quicksolve should say?

Answer on page 92.

72

19. Shortstop's Bike

Junior got off his bike and knocked on his friend Shortstop's front door. Shortstop was usually sitting on his bike in the driveway when Junior came by, and they would ride to school together each morning.

"Where's your bike?" Junior asked when Shortstop came to the door with his backpack in his hand and a sad look on his face.

"Somebody stole it from our garage yesterday afternoon," Shortstop said.

"Did you see anything?" Junior asked.

73

"No," Shortstop answered, "but my sister did. She heard a noise and looked out the window just in time to see a kid riding off on my bike. She doesn't know who it was, though. She only saw his back. She said he had on a denim jacket. It could have been anyone."

"We can check the bikes at school," Junior said as he pushed his bike down the sidewalk beside Shortstop.

Prissy Powers was standing by the long row of bikes behind the school. "Hi, Junior. Hi, Shortstop. How come you're walking?"

"My bike was stolen yesterday," Shortstop said.

"I think we'll find it," Junior said confidently as he walked down the long row of bikes, stroking the crossbar of the first one of many that looked like Shortstop's.

"But there are so many that are just alike, even yours," Prissy said to Junior.

"That's good," Junior said, moving down the row to the next bike like Shortstop's.

76

Why did Junior say that?

Answer on page 93.

20.
120 Hippopotamuses

Grandpa parked in front of Joe's Barbershop on Main Street across from an alley. Junior and his twin cousins got out of the car. Junior didn't know Flora and Fauna were setting him up. They wanted to see if he was smart enough to be considered one of the family.

Junior was startled for a second when he saw a young girl standing in front of the barbershop wearing bib-overall shorts and a white T-shirt that matched the outfits the twins wore.

"Hi, Bobbi," Fauna said. "Grandpa and our cousin Junior are getting haircuts. Why don't we walk down the street and get some ice cream?"

"You three look like you're on a team," Grandpa said, unwittingly falling into stride with the girls.

"We do like to run together," Bobbi said.

78

"Are you good runners?" Junior asked.

"Fauna is the fastest girl in the world," Flora said. "She can run around that block in two minutes."

Junior looked up and down the street, making his own estimation. "That's hard to believe," he said.

"Bet you an ice cream," Flora said.

"Okay," Junior agreed.

"You start counting hippopotamuses when she starts running. Fauna will be back here before you can count 120 hippopotamuses. Bobbi and I will go up the alley and make sure she doesn't cheat. We can do it while you're getting a haircut. You can watch from the barbershop," Flora said.

"I think I read a story like this once," Junior said.

Flora looked worried for a second. "Was it Chariots of Fire?" she asked.

"I don't think so," Junior answered, "but I'm going to enjoy the free ice cream.

80

What has Junior figured out?

Answer on page 93.

21. DNA

Shortstop sat at his desk in his garage with a shocked look on his face. He was looking at a note he had just received in the mail. The note was made of letters cut from a magazine and pasted to a sheet of paper to form the words "I will get you." His hands were surprisingly steady as he took scissors from the desk drawer and carefully cut the stamp off the envelope. He laid the stamp on his desk next to the envelope and letter. Then he picked up the cordless phone he had brought from the house. He stepped out onto his driveway and into the sunlight to be closer to the receiver in the house as he punched in Junior Quicksolve's phone number.

"Junior?" he said into the phone. "I just got a threatening letter in the mail. It's written with letters pasted on a piece

81

of paper. I think it's from John Bigdood. I know he's mad at me because I reported him for starting a fight. He probably wiped off his fingerprints, but what about DNA? Can't your dad get a stamp tested? I heard you can tell who licked it by their DNA."

Shortstop couldn't hear Junior's response clearly, so he stepped onto his back porch and into the house. He heard a noise behind him as he closed the door. "Wait!" he shouted. "John Bigdood just ran into my garage and took something off my desk!"

Shortstop ran outside and into the garage. "Oh, no!" he said, exasperated, as he walked back into the house.

Then he laughed.

"What happened?" Junior asked.

"He took the envelope from my desk, but he left the stamp and the letter. He must have been hiding beside the garage to see my reaction to the note. He probably heard what I said and grabbed the envelope when he had the chance. I don't know why he didn't take the stamp, too. We can still prove it was him with that," Shortstop said.

"I don't think we would find his DNA on that stamp even if Dad could get someone to test it," Junior said. "But we don't need it now, anyway. He has proven he was the one."

How has John Bigdood proven his guilt?

Answer on page 94.

84

Answers

1. **Small Change**—The young man was on the phone making a local call for 20 minutes. Junior and Dr. Quicksolve knew he should not have needed to put more money in as they came in. They figured he was getting rid of the evidence. Dr. Quicksolve wants the phone company to open the coin box to find the missing dimes.

2. **High Voltage**—Junior knew Voltage was a science teacher, and he remembered something he had learned in science class when he looked at the table. Lemon juice makes good invisible ink, and you can use a toothpick to write with it. Sure enough, when he passed a lighted match under the sheet of paper, the words "YASEPH'S COTTAGE" appeared. Lieutenant Rootumout sent some offcers to Yaseph's

cottage in the mountains where they rescued Mr. Voltage.

3. Early Morning Crime—Junior suspects John Bigdood. He has his drumsticks as an excuse to wear his band gloves, which cover his hands so no one can see the red stains from the pistachio shells on his fingers.

4. Hopalong—Dusty said Slim had just raised his leg to the stirrup to mount his horse. He also said the killer turned to his right as he came out of the saloon. If both things are true, a man exiting the saloon like that could not have shot Slim because his horse would have been between him and the saloon door. Dusty must be lying.

5. Five-Finger Discount—Junior thought John Bigdood took the CD out of the store on purpose, setting off the alarm while Bobby Socks left the store on the other side of the wide door at the same time with other stolen merchandise. Since John returned what he had taken and left without causing the alarm to go off, the clerk thought everything was all right.

6. **I'd Rather Owe You**—If Lyle had been knocked down and then wrestled with the dog as he said, not only would he have dropped the money, he would also have dropped his Super Slop Icy.

7. **Frontiersman**—Junior thought Blowhard was confused for several reasons you may have guessed. He seemed confused about a couple of Western heroes—Buffalo Bill Cody and Wild Bill Hickok. It was Wild Bill Hickok who

served as a scout for Lieutenant George Custer. He didn't die at Custer's Last Stand, though. Ironically, he did die that same year (1876), when he was shot in the back in a saloon. (Kit Carson died several years before that.) It was Buffalo Bill Cody who rode for the pony express in 1860, when he was only 14 or 15 years old. (Kit Carson would have been a little old for that job at 51.) Finally, it was also Buffalo Bill who was awarded the Congressional Medal of Honor, only to have it taken away because he was a civilian.

8. **Egyptian Mystery**—Junior learned a little about the ancient Egyptian writing called hieroglyphics. He knew the "coiled rope" symbol, which looks similar to a nine, represents 100. Two of these would mean 200. Since the curator lived in apartment 202, Junior figured that the victim was indicating that

the assailant was his neighbor in apartment 200.

9. Junior's Mystery Puzzle—1) There is no June 31. 2) He had been sitting there for hours, yet he said his glasses became foggy. There is no reason for that to happen. 3) He said his brother wasn't in town. Then he said he went straight to his brother's apartment and talked to him. 4) He said he put a clip into his revolver. You put a clip of bullets into an automatic pistol, but not normally into a revolver. 5) He said it had been raining for days, yet the convertible top was down when the car was in the driveway.

10. A Young Hero—Junior thought his dad could have tied the jump rope to the hula hoop and lowered it to the little girl. She could just sit in the hoop like on a swing

while she was slowly pulled up.
He was right.

11. Australian Adventure—The story is hard to believe, even if you don't know that Australia has no ferocious wild bears.

12. Shortstop's Business—Junior was talking about looking out the window and up at Stephen's telescope. He thought Stephen could have used his telescope to read the combination to Junior's safe. When he saw Junior at the computer, he came in quietly and took the money. He didn't even have to go back out of the house. He just pretended to come in shouting a warning to Junior.

13. Classroom Crime—If Bobby was only in the room a minute and used that time to wash his hands, the sink would be wet. If he is lying, and he took time to steal the money, the sink would be dry.

14. **Strikeout**—Junior thinks Homer should not be trusted because he sells counterfeit baseball cards. Mickey Mantle played for the Yankees in 1951, so there cannot be a 1953 rookie card.

15. **Socks**—Bobby said they were playing a team from Jackson. That means his was the home team, which would bat second and wouldn't bat the last inning if they were ahead after the visitors' last bat.

16. **Buz**—Buz's story about catching bees was his alibi for being out in the field with the jar. He doesn't really

know much about bees. He made the common mistake of calling the large black-and-yellow bumblebee a yellow jacket, even though it is actually not a bee but a small wasp.

17. Shadow Heart Trail—The voice on the walkie-talkie said they were two and a half miles down the trail and they turned toward the morning sun. They must have turned right toward the east.

18. The Real McCoy—Junior knew Blowhard's story about "the real McCoy" was not true. It is generally accepted that the expression is connected to an invention that automatically lubricates moving parts on many kinds of machine. The inventor was an African-American named Elijah McCoy.

19. Shortstop's Bike—Because there are so many bikes that look alike, the thief would probably think it was safe to ride it to school, believing Shortstop could not identify his bike. Junior and Shortstop had wisely etched their names inconspicuously under the crossbars of their bikes where no one would notice, but Junior could feel the engraving with his fingers.

20. 120 Hippopotamuses—Junior thinks Fauna will start the race while Flora and Bobbi wait at the other end of the alley. Even before Fauna has had enough time to round the corner out of sight, Flora will start running the second half of the race. After Flora finishes the race, Fauna will come down the alley with Bobbi, and they will say it was a fair race.

21. DNA—Junior figured John proved his guilt by taking just the envelope and ignoring the stamp. Only the guilty person would know his DNA would not be on the stamp because it was a self-adhesive, peel-off stamp, which, unlike the envelope, didn't need to be licked.

About the Author

Jim Sukach has taught middle school English for 20 years. He has also studied the British educational system at first hand, and has a master's degree in Educational Psychology, a subject he has also taught at Eastern Michigan University. The author of many successful books, most of them featuring Dr.Quicksolve, including Quicksolve Whodunit Puzzles; Baffling Whodunit Puzzles; Challenging Whodunit Puzzles; Great Quicksolve Whodunit Puzzles; Clever Quicksolve Whodunit Puzzles; Wicked Whodunits, and Crime-Scene Whodunits, he lives in the Ann Arbor, Michigan area.

Index